JEDBURGH ABBEY

Richard Fawcett

Principal Inspector of Ancient Monuments

Edited by Chris Tabraham

Principal photography by David Henrie

Designed by HMSO Graphic Design
Edinburgh

For many people Jedburgh Abbey is memorable chiefly as a dramatically sited monument viewed soon after their arrival in Scotland. Perhaps it was always intended to be seen as such. By founding it here, David I was demonstrating that his control extended up to the English Border. He was also impressing upon the English that the Scots were able to build on the grand scale.

The abbey church was started soon after 1138 for a community of Augustinian canons. Parts of the original choir and transepts still survive, but much of the rest of this magnificent building dates from a campaign begun in about 1180 and extending into the early thirteenth century. Following completion of the church, the monastic buildings around the open cloister garden on its south side were progressively laid out to the plan customary for a religious establishment.

Though Jedburgh was founded in an age when the two kingdoms were at peace, her position on the Border was to prove a major cause of suffering to the community it housed. As Anglo-Scottish relations deteriorated from 1296, the abbey was exposed as a natural target. Around 1305 the English removed part of the lead roofing and further damage was suffered in 1410, 1416 and 1464. But it was the devastating English attacks of 1523, 1544 and 1545 which dealt blows from which there was no real recovery. Fortunately, the church was spared further devastation after the Reformation in 1560 for it continued to be used by the local community as its parish church. It was that use, until 1875, which ensured that the abbey church at Jedburgh still stands as the best-preserved of the four Border abbeys.

This booklet provides a short tour around the abbey, followed by short accounts of its historical background and of the structural story of its best-preserved building, the church. It is hoped that the booklet, read in conjunction with the display material placed around the abbey, will help visitors to understand and enjoy what they see.

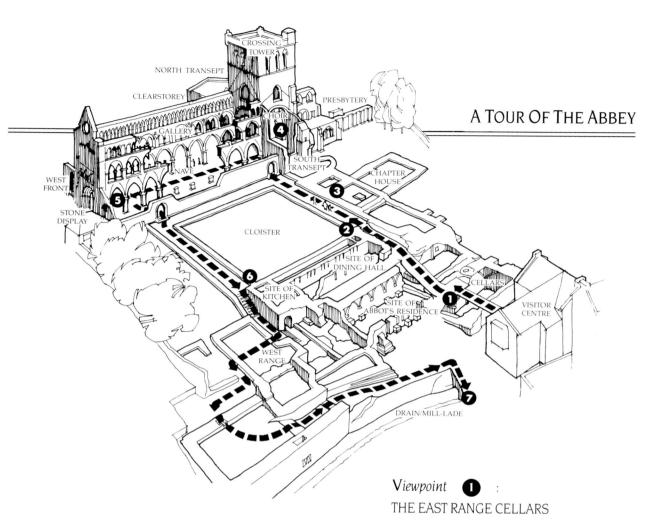

NORTH TRANSEPT

CLEARSTOREY

CROSSING TOWER

PRESBYTERY

GALLERY

CHOIR

NAVE

SOUTH TRANSEPT

CHAPTER HOUSE

WEST FRONT

STONE DISPLAY

CLOISTER

SITE OF DINING HALL

SITE OF KITCHEN

SITE OF ABBOT'S RESIDENCE

CELLARS

VISITOR CENTRE

WEST RANGE

DRAIN/MILL-LADE

Viewpoint **1** :
THE EAST RANGE CELLARS

The tour of the abbey begins at the visitor centre, where a glimpse into the life of the community of Augustinian canons may be found. Artefacts found during excavation in 1984 shed a little light on the character and life-style of the community that lived and worked here.

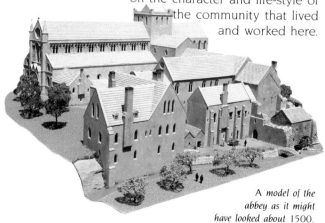

A model of the abbey as it might have looked about 1500.

The terraced river-side site chosen for the abbey meant that the buildings closer to the Jed Water had to be raised on undercrofts or basements. Those beneath the east range, which were probably built in the later thirteenth century, served as storage cellars. The canons' dormitory was on the second floor above the main cloister level. At the outer end of the dormitory was the latrine block or reredorter, flushed by water channelled into a drain leading off the river. By the fourteenth century the undercroft had been abandoned, possibly as a result of war damage, and a crude wall was built across it. Beyond this cross wall a corn mill was eventually built, its wheel powered by the water which had previously flushed the drains. That mill lade continued to provide power until 1950 and still passes below the visitor centre.

Archaeological excavations in progress on the east range in 1984. The stone-lined graves beneath the floor of the chapter house are clearly visible in the foreground. The Jedburgh Comb and its associated artefacts (illustrated below) were discovered in a sewage ditch beside the east range (marked with an X).

The Jedburgh Comb (above) and its associated artefacts (right). The collection may be seen as the standard personal possessions of a well-to-do gentlemean of the early 12th century, probably someone of Anglo-Norman origin. The objects were lost or buried about the time construction work was beginning on the abbey church in 1138. The comb is a superb piece of craftsmanship, created from walrus ivory around 1100, possibly in southern England. It is carved on both faces. This face shows two mythical beasts in combat. The other objects are an ivory pendant, a horn buckle, a whetstone, a ceramic lamp-holder and a cooking pot.

Viewpoint ❷ :
THE CLOISTER

At the heart of the abbey was the rectangular open space known as the cloister. It lies on the south side of the abbey church, which dominated the whole complex. Along the four sides of the cloister were covered walks connecting the more important buildings of the abbey and providing sheltered space for the canons to read and write. On the east side of the cloister were several important rooms. Hard by the church was the parlour where the canons were permitted to converse on matters of importance, and which also served as a passageway or slype, to their burial ground. Next to this was the chapter-house (see Viewpoint 3). Further south was perhaps the warming house or calefactory, where the canons were allowed to gather around a fire in cold weather. Running over all these was their dormitory. The central court, or garth, of the cloister may have served as a garden tended by the canons. It has been laid out once again as a late-medieval garden, and selections of flowers, herbs and shrubs of the period now grow here. They include plants grown for their medicinal or culinary properties. Leading off the east and west walks of the cloister are the two processional doorways into the church. The eastern one is original and still shows the quality of craftsmanship produced by the Jedburgh masons in the 1180s. The western of these two doors is a reconstruction of 1876.

An impression of the east cloister walk, looking north towards the processional door leading to the church.

Viewpoint ❸ :
THE CHAPTER-HOUSE

The chapter-house was the meeting room of the community. At the daily gatherings here, sins were confessed – or accused – and the business of the abbey was discussed. Archaeological excavation in 1984 showed that the present square chamber was the third, and smallest, chapter-house on the site. The first, built along with the rest of the east range in the thirteenth century, was larger, projecting a short way east of the range. In time, this was extended even further, perhaps reflecting the time when the community had reached its greatest number. The square chamber we now see was contained entirely within the range. It bears comparison with chapter-houses at Crossraguel Abbey (Ayrshire) and Glenluce Abbey (Wigtonshire) and presumably dates to the same time – the later fifteenth century.

Stone-lined graves beneath the chapter-house floor containing the mortal remains of senior abbey officials.

Viewpoint ❹ :
THE EASTERN LIMB OF THE CHURCH

The eastern half of the church, housing the canons' stalls and high altar, is both the most fascinating and the most complex. The earliest portion is that immediately east of the crossing tower, where the lower storeys were probably started soon after 1138. Particularly worthy of note is the way in which the arcade and gallery stages are enveloped by arches carried on giant cylindrical columns.

Around 1180 the outer end of the eastern arm, the presbytery, was rebuilt to a rectangular plan, presumably to provide a more spacious setting for the high altar. Little now remains of this, although its pointed Gothic arches and delicately carved capitals provide an interesting contrast with the bolder, semi-circular arches, chevron (zig-zag) decoration and scalloped capitals of the earlier work.

The north transept, originally accommodating side altars, was extended and re-modelled by Bishop William Turnbull of Glasgow (1447–54). In 1681, it was appropriated by the Kerr family and walled off as their burial place. Under abbots John Hall (1478–84) and Thomas Cranston (1484–88) there was much rebuilding below the tower and in adjacent areas; their arms or names are found at several points on the rebuilt or remodelled tower piers and in the chapels flanking the choir.

Crudely-built walls under the east tower arch and cutting off the outer end of the south transept are probably the consequences of damage control operations after English attacks in the early 16th century. They were retained when the parishioners continued to worship here after the Reformation.

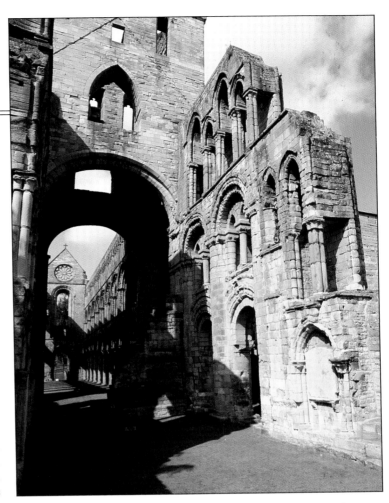

The eastern limb of the church, containing the presbytery and part of the canons' choir, looking west. The earliest part has two lofty arches which embrace the openings into the aisles and into the galleries above the aisles.

The initials of Abbot Thomas Cranston, together with a crozier, carved upon a reconstructed pier supporting the crossing tower.

The western limb of the church, the nave, looking from
below the crossing tower towards the west front with its
processional entrance doorway.

Viewpoint ⑤ :
THE WESTERN LIMB OF THE CHURCH

The nave, that part of the church always
open to lay folk, is a splendid structure
probably started in the 1180s and completed
early in the following century. It is most
remarkable for its structural completeness,
giving us an unparalleled impression of a
major Scottish abbey church at a most
important phase of architectural development, the transition from Romanesque to
Gothic. Visitors will find it rewarding to
examine the delightful details of the carved
capitals on the piers and columns of all
three stages, and on the doorways which
lead into the cloister. The west front, with
its processional portal and single window
flanked by decorative arcading, shows a
development of ideas employed earlier at
nearby Kelso, though the fine rose window
high up in the gable belongs to the fifteenth
century.

Fragment of a finely-carved
statue of around 1180, now
on show in the visitor centre.

Viewpoint ⑥ :
THE DINING HALL

The canons' dining hall, or refectory, was on
the south side of the cloister. At some stage
in the abbey's history, perhaps in the late
thirteenth century, when the number of
canons might have reached its peak, it was
decided to enlarge the cloister to south and
west. On the south side this was achieved
by diverting the cloister walk through the
range itself and by relocating the dining hall
at first-floor level above both a narrow
undercroft and the cloister walk itself.
Nothing now remains of the dining hall, but
a drain formerly serving the lavatory, or
washing place, where the canons washed
their hands before eating, can still be seen.
At the west end of the dining hall are the
foundations of the kitchens and other
domestic offices which served it.

Viewpoint ⑦ :
THE WEST RANGE AND THE
OUTER BUILDINGS ON THE SOUTH SIDE

The west cloister range presumably housed
buildings requiring contact with the outside
world. Here was accommodation for the
cellarer, who was responsible for the pro-
visions, the almoner, who looked after the
poor, and the guest-master, who provided
hospitality for travellers. At Jedburgh, sadly,
virtually nothing survives of this range. All
we have is a large block of uncertain use
at its southern end, adjacent to the kitchen
area.

To the south of the south range, between
the dining hall and the river, is an undercroft
of late thirteenth-century date traditionally
identified with the infirmary, where sick and
old monks lived in easier circumstances than
would have prevailed for the rest of the
community. It was unusual, though, to have
the infirmary in such a position, and its
situation and superlative architecture suggest that it may have been the basement
of the abbot's residence. In this position the
abbot could still be seen to be living com-
munally with the canons, albeit at arms'
length and with the independence his rank
and status in time came to expect of him.

Part of a shrine (8th century AD), designed to hold the body of a saint, found during clearance work earlier this century and now on display in the visitor centre.

A crudely-carved stone (9th or 10th century AD), found during excavation in 1984 and appearing to depict Christ in His Majesty above tormented souls.

THE EARLY COMMUNITY

Jedburgh's history as a religious community may stretch back to around AD 830, when Bishop Ecgred of Lindisfarne built a church at Gedwearde (Jedworth). Little is known about the community it housed until about 1080, when Eadulph Rus, one of the murderers of Bishop Walcher of Durham, was buried for a short time within its church. His remains were later unceremoniously dug up and disposed of. Indeed, we cannot even be entirely certain where the early church was, since we know that Ecgred founded two settlements within a few miles of each other, both with the name of Jedworth. However, the finding of a considerable number of early carved stones around the abbey, together with a quantity of Anglo-Saxon coins, would suggest that it was on this site that the early community had been established.

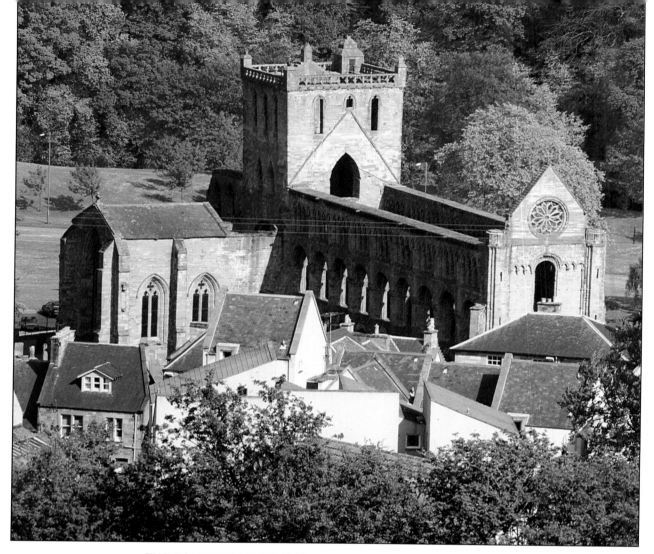

THE FOUNDATION OF THE AUGUSTINIAN COMMUNITY

The abbey from the north west. In the foreground is the long western limb, the nave. To the left is the northern of the two cross arms, the transepts. Rising above the heart of the church is the bell tower.

Jedburgh was founded at a stage of tremendous activity in the religious life of medieval Scotland. After a long period during which monastic life had virtually disappeared, the kingdom was ruled by a succession of monarchs who appreciated both the political and the spiritual advantages of a healthy Church. The most active of these, David I (1124–53), had spent much of his early years at the court of his brother-in-law, Henry I of England, where he had been greatly impressed by the vigour and architectural magnificence of the abbeys. Henry had granted vast estates to David through marriage to England's greatest heiress, the daughter of the earl of Northumbria, and

this allowed him to develop a taste for patronage of the religious orders which never left him.

Jedburgh was founded jointly by David and his former teacher, Bishop John of Glasgow, in about 1138. First established as a priory, with a prior as its head, by about 1154 its status had been raised to that of an abbey. It eventually came to have the priories of Blantyre (Lanarkshire), Canonbie (Dumfriesshire) and Restenneth (Angus) dependent upon it.

The foundation of Jedburgh was part of David's policy of using the reorganisation of the Church as a means of enforcing order on the unruly kingdom he inherited from his brother in 1124. But, in reorganising the Church within his kingdom, he had to struggle against the archbishop of York,

who claimed authority over it. Jedburgh's position close to the Border with England was probably significant for its re-establishment may be connected with Bishop John's return to his diocese in 1138, after a particularly bitter phase of the struggle with York and the papacy. John's love for Jedburgh was such that he chose to be buried here on his death in 1147.

Endowing a religious community was a costly business and David's efforts on behalf of the Church called for grants of royal property to an extent which dismayed later kings. Yet David was not alone in his benefactions. Others who wished to share in the merits of supporting the canons' prayers also made gifts. They included Randolph de Soules, the king's butler and lord of nearby Liddesdale, and William de Vieuxpont, lord of Westmorland in England. By the Reformation the abbey enjoyed a very considerable annual income. Apart from land, a favoured form of endowment was for a benefactor to grant a parish church which was in his patronage, with the assumption that the main income of the parish would be appropriated. Jedburgh eventually possessed about twenty such churches.

THE AUGUSTINIAN CANONS

David I had a comprehensive knowledge of the various religious orders which were emerging in that period of fervent renewal, and he was responsible for introducing several of these into Scotland. At Jedburgh Augustinian canons were introduced, pos-sibly from the abbey of St Quentin near Beauvais in France. David may have become aware of St Quentin through his sister, Queen Matilda of England, since the priory of St Botolph in Colchester had apparently earlier sought guidance from St Quentin.

Canons regular, that is canons who fol-lowed a monastic rule or 'regula', were priests living a form of communal life. The Augustinians took their title from St Augustine of Hippo, who died in AD 430. In the eleventh century, groups of priests seeking a form of spiritual co-existence had looked to the writings of that saint for guidance and when they were formally recognised as a distinct order in 1059 they adopted him as their figurehead.

The Augustinians, or 'black canons' as they were known from the colour of their habit, were not as strictly organised as the orders of monks. They also tended to be less fully enclosed than the monks and, as priests, they frequently served the parishes granted to them. Nevertheless, their life was essentially like that of the monks and they were similarly bound by vows of poverty, chastity and obedience. The basis of their day was the 'work of God', a sequence of services of psalms, prayers and anthems, starting in the early hours of the morning and finishing in the evening, although their version of these services was probably rather shorter than that of the monks. Between these services were others, including one or more daily masses. There was also time for spiritual, intellectual or even manual activities.

The abbey floodlit.

Edward I of England.
"Hammer of the Scots"
(courtesy of the Dean and
Chapter of Lincoln
Cathedral).

THE ABBEY
AND THE WARS WITH ENGLAND

In 1285 the community played host to the second marriage of Alexander III, to Yolande de Dreux. According to legend, the ceremony was marred by a ghostly figure which foretold the king's death in the following year. It was that death, followed by the death four years later of his heir, his young grand-daughter, Margaret, the Maid of Norway, which was the prelude to the long and bloody Wars of Independence with England.

Jedburgh's position on the Border made it particularly vulnerable and in 1296 Edward I of England stayed here and engineered the election of a pro-English abbot. The abbey's first experience of violence came about nine years later, when lead from the roofs was removed. The abbey's English leanings at one stage irritated the more patriotic Scots, and in

1312 the abbot and eleven of his canons fled across the Border when the Scottish capture of Roxburgh Castle left them unprotected. The community was walking a tightrope between the two sides, and the massive spiritual effort of Abbot Kennock, who maintained peace for a decade through dint of prayer, calls for some admiration.

In the fifteenth century there were damaging attacks in 1410, 1416 and 1464. In 1476, when efforts were made to unite the priory of Restenneth with Jedburgh, the monastic buildings were said to be in need of repair, and by 1502 the situation had worsened. Although medieval reports on the state of buildings were usually exaggerated, rebuilding of parts of the church in the later fifteenth century graphically illustrates that much needed to be done. Worse was to come in the following century. In 1523 English forces under the earl of Surrey attacked and burned the abbey. It was again ravaged by English forces in 1544 and 1545, shortly before the final onslaught of the Reformation.

The arms of Abbot Cranston on a crossing tower pier rebuilt about 1480.

THE ABBEY AND THE REFORMATION

The impact of the wars with England seriously sapped the vitality of the abbeys on the Border. By 1545 there were probably no more than eight canons here at Jedburgh, and there is reason for believing that by then much of the original fervour of religious life had passed, although the deportment of the individual canons was doubtless seemly enough.

An additional factor was the appointment of commendators, rather than abbots, to head them. These were royal appointees granted the office as a reward for their services, and for most their chief aim was to establish an hereditary asset for their families. At Jedburgh the abbey came under the control of the Home family and, although John Home was properly elected abbot in 1512, by the 1520s part of the income was being directed to his nephew, Andrew. In 1606 parliament enacted that the abbey should form part of a lordship for Alexander Home. We know little about the circumstances of the canons themselves after the abolition of monastic life in 1560, but those who wished were probably allowed to remain in their old home until death took its final toll.

The abbey from the north in the 18th century. To the left are the presbytery and canons' choir, in a better state of preservation than today. To the right may be seen the nave when still in use as a parish church.

THE BUILDING OF THE ABBEY CHURCH

Like most major churches of the middle ages, Jedburgh abbey church was laid out on a cross-shaped plan, with its head towards the east. The eastern limb had the presbytery, containing the high altar at its furthest end. In front of this was the canons' choir, probably stretching down into part of the western limb. Projecting to either side of the choir were transepts or cross arms, providing lateral processional areas and housing additional altars. The western limb was the nave which, except for part of the canons' choir at its eastern end, was open to the lay folk. Above the junction of the main body of the church and the transepts was a bell tower.

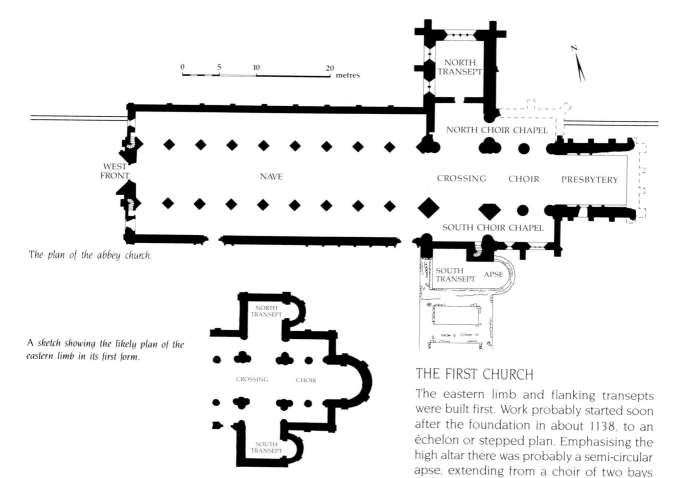

0 5 10   20 metres

The plan of the abbey church.

NORTH
TRANSEPT

NORTH CHOIR CHAPEL

WEST
FRONT

NAVE

CROSSING   CHOIR   PRESBYTERY

SOUTH CHOIR CHAPEL

SOUTH
TRANSEPT   APSE

A sketch showing the likely plan of the
eastern limb in its first form.

NORTH
TRANSEPT

CROSSING   CHOIR

SOUTH
TRANSEPT

The nave at Romsey abbey,
Hampshire, with giant piers
similar to those at Jedburgh.

THE FIRST CHURCH

The eastern limb and flanking transepts
were built first. Work probably started soon
after the foundation in about 1138, to an
échelon or stepped plan. Emphasising the
high altar there was probably a semi-circular
apse, extending from a choir of two bays
flanked by aisles; the transepts projected
one bay beyond the aisles, each with an
apse on its east side. The two eastern bays
of the nave were probably started at the
same time, to contain part of the canons'
choir and to provide structural support for
the crossing area, above which the tower
would eventually rise. However, the completion of the nave had to await further funds.

Of this first building campaign, the two
inner walls of the choir, the two northern
crossing piers, and parts of the transepts
survive most completely. These show that
the work was designed by a master mason
of high calibre, almost certainly brought to
Scotland at the request of David I himself.

The most noteworthy feature of the design
is the way in which the two lower storeys —
the arcade opening into the aisles and the
gallery above the aisles — are embraced by
single arches carried on giant columns. This
type of design is seen elsewhere in a group
of churches in western and southern England,

The first bays of the canons' choir, the earliest surviving part of the abbey church. This clearly shows how the giant arches embrace two tiers of openings.

of which Romsey Abbey in Hampshire, built in the early 1100s, is the best-known example. David knew Romsey, because his aunt, Christina, was a nun there, and his sister, Matilda, had stayed there before her marriage to Henry I in 1100.

However, the designer of Jedburgh may have come from Tewkesbury, in Gloucestershire, where this type of design with giant columns embracing two storeys probably first appeared after about 1087. From what we know of the choir there, it must have been very like what we now see at Jedburgh. It is now thought that Tewkesbury's choir originally had no clearstorey, or upper tier of windows, above the aisles and galleries; it is also thought that Tewkesbury could have been covered by a semi-circular stone barrel-vault. Similarly, at Jedburgh it is possible that at first the choir had no clearstorey and that there could have been a half-round timber ceiling – continuing the curve of the tower arch – to give it an appearance similar to Tewkesbury.

The abbey church in 1775, at which time more of the presbytery was preserved than now.

THE ENLARGEMENT OF THE PRESBYTERY

When this first phase of building operations was completed, there was a pause of some years before construction started again in the later decades of the twelfth century. The architectural evidence suggests that when work resumed, it was carried forward with tremendous pace, with two or more teams perhaps working simultaneously in different parts of the church.

The first part of the new campaign may have been the reconstruction of the presbytery to a rectangular plan, in the design

of which no attempt was made to match up with the choir bays. Above a low storey of solid walling embellished by decorative arches was a higher storey with a wall passage running in front of windows and with what must have been an elegant arcade towards the body of the presbytery. Such a design may be compared with the nunnery church of Nun Monkton in Yorkshire or the Benedictine priory church of Coldingham in Berwickshire, and a date around 1180 seems most likely for its construction.

As in the earlier bays of the choir, there may have been at first no intention of build-ing an upper rank of clearstorey windows. Nevertheless, it could have been soon after-wards that it was decided to add a clear-storey to both the eastern limb and transepts. On the north side of the choir there are traces of a lower clearstorey wall than the one we now see, next to the tower, and the stump of a similar clearstorey is also to be seen in the south transept. The surviving details suggest that both these clearstoreys represent additions to the original fabric, but it is possible that the first of them was not completed before the decision was taken to replace it by a higher one.

A reconstruction sketch of the eastern limb as it may have appeared after the presbytery had been lengthened but before a clearstorey had been added above this part of the church.

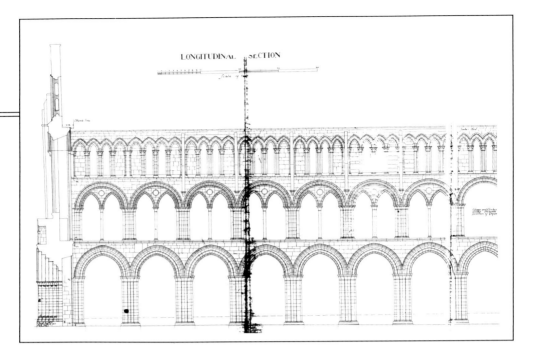

LONGITUDINAL SECTION

A measured drawing of the north side of the nave, illustrating its horizontal division into three storeys.

THE DESIGN OF THE NAVE

The nave was probably started soon after the remodelling of the presbytery, in the 1180s, and was planned on an even grander scale than the earlier parts. It was divided into nine bays flanked by an aisle on each side and was three full storeys in height. Piers with eight lobes of keeled or pointed profile carried the richly-moulded arches opening into the aisles. Above these were

An elaborate water-leaf cap on the nave arcade.

A water-leaf cap at Byland Abbey, Yorkshire, showing a similar approach to design as at Jedburgh.

tall galleries with a round-arched opening subdivided by two pointed arches in each bay. Lighting the central part was the clearstorey, with two windows set in a continuous arcade of four arches to each bay.

The overall design, along with the carving on the capitals of the piers, shows that the nave is one of a group of buildings in northern England and lowland Scotland which were much influenced by ideas introduced into the area by the Cistercian order of monks. Jedburgh's own master mason may have come from St Andrews, where the greatest of Scottish cathedrals had been started soon after 1160, and which also housed a community of Augustinian canons. Nevertheless, many individuals must have played a part in the construction, and some of the masons who carved the decorative details may have come from north Yorkshire. Some of the capitals carved with variants of the foliage known as water leaf, for example, show similarities with carving at the Cistercian abbey of Byland.

Comparison of the nave and the earliest part of the choir provides a valuable pointer to architectural changes over the forty years separating the design of the two parts. Whereas the choir was designed to give an

The upper storeys of the nave: the tall galleries above the aisle vaults, and the row of arches opening onto the wall passages in front of the clearstorey windows.

appearance of great structural weight and strength, in the nave the masonry appears to be supported with effortless ease, despite the greater masses of stone. This is achieved largely through the treatment of the mouldings of the arches and their supports, which are thinner and more linear in effect, and also by the way in which these mouldings seem to contain the areas of masonry. These give it a feeling of weightlessness. The aims of the masons who designed the two parts were very different: the first designed in the Romanesque idiom of his time, whereas the second was playing his part in the introduction of the Gothic style.

The nave of the abbey church.

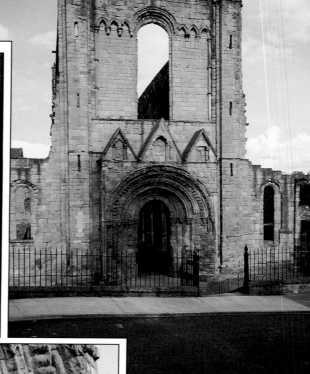

The west doorway.

A detail of the carved decoration of the west doorway. This may originally have been richly coloured.

The design of the magnificent processional entrance doorway in the west wall suggests that the west end was the first part of the nave to be started. Above the shafts flanking the door are bird-like creatures and carved capitals ultimately inspired by the Corinthian capitals of the Romans. The arches and jambs, or flanks, were decorated with variants of chevron, or zig-zag, ornament and similar decoration was used in the processional doorways from the cloister. The upper parts of the west front may have been designed by a mason who had previously worked at Kelso Abbey, which has a simpler version of the tall single window flanked by decorative arcading.

In building the nave, the existing parts would have been left undisturbed as long as possible. Slight differences in the bases of the two eastern piers show these were built last, and suggest that part of the earlier building had to be removed once the rest of the nave was complete. Other changes, such as a mid-height change in the two spiral staircases of the west front, point to a pause in the operations when the gallery was completed. The design of the nave clearstorey may have been modified about the same time.

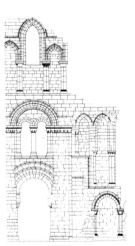

A reconstruction of the eastern limb of the church after the addition of the clearstorey above the original wall head.

A measured drawing of part of the south side of the eastern limb.

THE CLEARSTOREYS OF THE NAVE AND CHOIR

The clearstorey of the nave was probably only completed in the thirteenth century. Subtle changes in the design of its capitals, such as the polygonal shape of their abaci (the top plate-like stones), point to the changing fashions which were progressively introduced at the turn of the twelfth and thirteenth centuries. But even before the nave clearstorey was started, it is likely that the decision was taken to replace the low clearstorey added to the eastern limb by a taller one. By doing this the total height of the choir and presbytery was raised to the same height as the nave. Curiously, there appears to have been no thought of raising the transept clearstorey at this time, so that, although the main body of the abbey church was of uniform height to either side of the tower, the cross arms were lower.

With the completion of the clearstorey over the nave, the abbey church was structurally complete for the first time, and attention must then have turned to the construction of the canons' domestic buildings. It is unlikely that major changes were made to it for over two centuries, apart from repairs necessitated by attacks in the course of the wars with England.

The north transept as rebuilt in the mid 15th century. It was probably originally intended to be covered by a stone vault and a more steeply-pointed roof.

BUILDING OPERATIONS IN THE FIFTEENTH CENTURY

The first major building works at the abbey church following its completion involved the reconstruction of the north transept to an enlarged rectangular plan. This was presumably to house additional altars and possibly also to make good damage suffered in the English attacks of 1410 and 1416. With its blank eastern wall to accommodate elaborate altarpieces and the large traceried windows in its northern and western walls, it was characteristic of Scottish architecture of the later fifteenth century. Traditionally, this operation has been attributed to Bishop William Turnbull of Glasgow (1447–54) on the basis of now-indecipherable arms above the north window. Since this window is virtually identical with one at Melrose, erected by Abbot Andrew Hunter (1444–1471), it is very likely that Turnbull was indeed respon-

sible for it. It seems there may have been an intention to raise the walls of the transept and place a stone vault over it, although it is unlikely that it was ever completed.

Bishop Turnbull also remodelled the chapel on the south side of the choir, which bears his arms, although this was again refashioned soon afterwards by Abbot John Hall (1478–84). It may be that the west gable was another part of the building altered around this time; its handsome rose window is very similar to a window in the west gable of the refectory at Dryburgh Abbey.

The later fifteenth century also saw major reconstruction around the crossing area, work perhaps necessitated by an English attack in 1464. Abbots John Hall (1478–84) and Thomas Cranston (1484–88) reconstructed the piers beneath the south side of the tower and strengthened the whole structure around the crossing. It is possible

The crossing area from the south. The construction of the stone vault over the south transept necessitated blocking an existing clearstorey, a fragment of which can be seen on the east side of the transept.

to identify much of their work from the presence of their names, initials and arms. Following on from this operation was the reconstruction of the central tower, which was completed by Archbishop Robert Blackadder of Glasgow (1483–1508) whose arms are at the wall-head. It was perhaps around the same time that a stone barrel-vault was built over the south transept.

FINAL BUILDING OPERATIONS

The final medieval building works were prob-ably a last, desperate attempt to contain the damage wrought by the English attacks of 1523 and 1544–5. It was possibly after the first attack that lower roofs were built over the nave and its aisles, the evidence for which may be seen on the tower, against the transepts, and in the slots and mouldings on the backs of the gallery arches. The modified appearance can have been nothing other than ungainly.

It may have been after the later attacks that the outer part of the south transept and the choir were walled off, in order to form a temporary church within the crossing and transept area. However, it is doubtful if the community had the resources to undertake more extensive repairs. After the Reforma-tion in 1560 it was this area which was first taken over as a makeshift parish church.

The ruined abbey from the Jed Water in 1793. By this time more than two centuries had passed since the Reformation, but part of the crumbling edifice's nave is still in use as a parish kirk (note the glazing inserted into the gallery arcade). The residence partly masking the kirk was the manse.

AFTER THE REFORMATION

Since the abbey church at Jedburgh had served the local parishioners as well as the canons, it continued to be used for worship after the Reformation. It seems likely, however, that only part of the area beneath the central tower and transepts (cross arms) was fully usable, and it was in this area that a new parish church was formed. By 1574 Privy Council records show that the roof of even this part was in advanced decay and it was proposed to remove the roof from the dining hall to repair it.

The choir of Jedburgh Old Parish Church before the restored west processional doorway around 1880.

There were further alarms in 1636 when one of the crossing-tower piers was judged to be at risk, and in 1642 the royal master mason, John Mylne, was asked to give his advice on the problem. Little was then done but between 1668 and 1671 a new church was created in the five western bays of the nave, with a roof at gallery level, rather than at the original wall-head (see the illustration on page 11). In 1681, much of the north transept was walled off by the Kerr family, the ancestors of the marquesses of Lothian, who had long used it as their burial place.

The major turning point in the church's modern history was the decision in 1875 to build a new parish church on the other side of the Jed Water, largely at the behest of the ninth marquess of Lothian. He subsequently paid for major repairs to the ancient fabric, and in 1913 the ruin was placed in the guardianship of HM Office of Works. Jedburgh was the first of the great Border abbeys to pass into state care.

FURTHER READING

For further information about the history and architecture of Jedburgh Abbey, the following are recommended:

Ian B Cowan and David Easson, *Medieval Religious Houses: Scotland* (1976).

James Watson, *Jedburgh Abbey and the abbeys of Teviotdale* (1894).

Royal Commission on the Ancient and Historical Monuments of Scotland, *Roxburghshire Inventory*, vol 2 (1956).

John Higgit, "The Jedburgh Comb", in *Romanesque and Gothic: Essays for George Zarnecki* (1987).

Tessa Garton, "The transitional sculpture of Jedburgh Abbey", in *Romanesque and Gothic: Essays for George Zarnecki* (1987).